C&M
VOL. 23

COVERS
USAF RF-4C &
USMC RF-4B VARIANTS

COLORS & MARKINGS OF THE

RECON
PHANTOMS

A DETAIL & SCALE AVIATION PUBLICATION

in detail & scale

Bert Kinzey & Ray Leader

KALMBACH BOOKS

Airlife Publishing Ltd.

England

 Published by Kalmbach Publishing Company, 21027 Crossroads Circle, P. O. Box 1612, Waukesha, Wisconsin 53187.

CONTRIBUTORS AND SOURCES:

BG James Brown, ANG (Ret.)
LTC Jerry Daily, Alabama ANG
Jim Leslie
Eddy de Kruyff
Nick Mills
Jim Rotramel
Naoki Nishimura
Wayne Whited
Mike Grove
Ben Knowles
Roy Lock
Don Logan
Doug Slowiak
Peter Wilson
Bob Leavitt
Bill Malerba
Dave Ostrowski
Steve Zinc
Jeff Rankin-Lowe
Lee Bracken
Craig Kaston
Mike Campbell
Brian Rogers
Peter Greve
Phillip Huston
Ian MacPherson
Daniel Soulaine
Dennis Jenkins
Charles Arrington
Robert Greby
David Prettyman
Steve Miller
Bob Stewart
Hideki Nagakubo
Mick Roth
Steve Daniels
Don Spering/A.I.R.
Aviation Photography of Miami
Flightleader
GB Aircraft Slides
Picciani Aircraft Slides
Select Air Productions
Centurion Enterprises
Military Aircraft Photographs
117th Reconnaissance Wing
106th Reconnaissance Squadron, Alabama ANG
U. S. Air Force
Department of Defense

FIRST PRINTING

Published in United States by
Kalmbach Publishing Co.
21027 Crossroads Circle
P.O. Box 1612
Waukesha, Wisconsin, 53187

Library of Congress Cataloging-in-Publication Data

Kinzey, Bert.
Colors & markings of recon Phantoms / Bert Kinzey & Ray Leader.
p. cm. -- (C&M ; vol. 23)
"Covers USAF RF-4C & USMC RF-4B variants."
"A Detail & Scale aviation publication."
ISBN 0-89024-221-6

1. Phantom II (Jet fighter plane) 2. Airplanes, Military--United States--Identification marks. 3. Reconniassance aircraft--United States. I. Leader, Ray. II. Title. III. Title: Colors and markings of Recon Phantoms. IV. Title: Recon Phantoms. V. Series.

UG1242.R4K5484 1994 358.4'483'0973
QBI94-677

Published in Great Britain
by Airlife Publishing Ltd.
7 St. John's Hill, Shrewsbury, SY1 1JE

British Library Cataloging in Publication Data

A catalog record for this book
is available from the British Library.

***Front cover:** Don Spering's beautiful artwork on RF-4C, 64-1041, commemorates the thirty-fifth anniversary of the first Phantom's initial flight. The aircraft belongs to the 106th Reconnaissance Squadron of the Alabama Air National Guard. This unit is part of the 117th Reconnaissance Wing, also based at Birmingham, Alabama. Additional photographs of this aircraft appear on page 39. (Spering/A.I.R.)*

***Rear cover, top photograph:** In honor of America's Bi-centennial Anniversary, VMFP-3 applied these beautiful red, white, and blue markings to one of their RF-4Bs, and the aircraft was named "Spirit of America." This photograph was taken in September 1976. (Roth)*

***Rear cover, bottom photograph:** RF-4C, 66-0440, was operated by the 15th Tactical Reconnaissance Squadron of the 18th Tactical Fighter Wing when this photograph was taken in October 1985. It is shown here with special markings that were applied for the reconnaissance meet known as Photo Finish 1985. Note the Shogun warrior on the inlet. (Whited)*

INTRODUCTION

An RF-4B from VMCJ-1 shows off the original Light Gull Gray over white paint scheme and colorful markings. The entire vertical tail is a very dark green, and the tail code is yellow. The squadron's insignia appears on both sides of the tail.
(Flightleader)

For over a quarter of a century, the F-4 Phantom served as a front line fighter for the U. S. Navy, Marines, and Air Force. Other Phantoms were exported to foreign nations or built under license in Asia and Europe. As a result, the F-4 became one of the most widely used and popular combat aircraft in aviation history. It was considered by many to be the premier fighter of its day, and it served admirably in combat. From Vietnam to Desert Storm, Phantoms flew almost every conceivable mission a fighter could perform. But ironically it was the RF-4B and RF-4C reconnaissance variants which remained operational with the Marines and Air Force longer than any of the eight major fighter variants used by these services. This book is the most extensive reference ever published which covers the paint schemes and markings used on these reconnaissance Phantoms.

The first production RF-4C made its initial flight on 18 May, 1964, and by October 1965, the Air Force was flying RF-4Cs on reconnaissance missions in Vietnam. More than twenty-five years later, RF-4Cs returned to war as they deployed to the Middle East for Operations Desert Shield and Desert Storm. In the interim, the Air Force used no less than five official paint schemes and a wide variety of markings on its recon Phantoms. A number of unofficial schemes were used on test and evaluation RF-4Cs as well. When this book was released in 1994, RF-4Cs were still in service with the Air National Guard. It seems certain that the operational life of this recon Phantom will exceed thirty years before the last RF-4C is retired.

The first flight by an RF-4B was made on 12 March 1965, and the Marines began combat operations with VMCJ-1 in Vietnam the following year. The last RF-4Bs were retired in 1990 before the Gulf War, but during the twenty-five years that the RF-4B served with the Marines, it was painted in three different official paint schemes, and some very interesting markings were applied to the aircraft. These ranged from colorful markings used in honor of the American Bi-centennial to subdued tactical markings that were almost invisible at any distance from the aircraft.

This book illustrates the paint schemes and markings applied to the recon Phantoms used by the Air Force and Marines on a unit-by-unit basis. Coverage begins on the next page with an explanation of the various official paint schemes used by these two services. Photographs and drawings illustrate the various camouflage patterns, and Federal Standard numbers are provided for the colors.

Because the RF-4C preceeded the RF-4B in service, we begin our unit-by-unit coverage with that variant. Each active Air Force wing that has operated the RF-4C is covered beginning on page 10. In most cases, RF-4Cs were flown by Tactical Reconnaissance Wings, but they were assigned to four Tactical Fighter Wings as well. Regardless of wing type, the active Air Force wings are arranged in numerical order. These are followed by four Air Force test and evaluation units which are also arranged in numerical order. The Ogden Air Logistics Center at Hill Air Force Base, Utah, comes next, followed by each of the eleven Air National Guard squadrons that have flown the RF-4C. The Guard units are arranged alphabetically by state. Finally the four Marine squadrons that flew the RF-4B are covered in numerical order. The photographs on the final page of this book illustrate the special markings used by VMFP-3 when the last RF-4Bs were retired in August 1990. As is the case with all of the books in the Colors & Markings Series, a special effort has been made to show commander's aircraft and those with special markings for reconnaissance meets and other events.

This extensive coverage of recon Phantoms would not have been possible without the help of the many contributors named on page 2. A special word of thanks is owed to Don Spering who has commemorated the Phantom's history through his beautiful artwork on a number of aircraft. Among them is the RF-4C which appears on the front cover of this book.

RECON PHANTOM PAINT SCHEMES

Early RF-4Cs were delivered to the U. S. Air Force in the Navy's Light Gull Gray over white paint scheme. All of the undersides of the aircraft were white, as were the upper surfaces of the flaps and ailerons. The rudder was also white unless painted over by unit markings. The inner panels of the horizontal stabilators were natural metal, however the outer surfaces were white on both the top and bottom sides. *(DOD)*

When the U. S. Air Force decided to add the Phantom to its inventory, it was obvious that the large powerful aircraft offered improved performance capabilities over any other fighter that was then in operation. In air-to-air combat, the F-4 proved to be better than the F-106 in most respects, and it was superior to the F-105 as a fighter-bomber. But Air Force planners also realized early on that the Phantom's airframe could easily be modified into an excellent tactical reconnaissance platform as well. In fact, the Specific Operational Requirements (SOR) for the RF-4C were issued almost three months prior to the SOR for the F-4C fighter variant. Recognizing the wisdom of the Air Force's decision to build a reconnaissance version of the Phantom, the Navy then placed an order for forty-six RF-4Bs for use with the Marines.

The first YRF-4C prototype made its initial flight on 8 August, 1963, and the first production RF-4C made its maiden flight on 18 May, 1964. By contrast, the first RF-4B did not fly until 12 March, 1965.

Because it already had experience with the Phantom and the McDonnell Aircraft Corporation, the Navy placed the initial orders for the F-4C and RF-4C on behalf of the Air Force. No other paint scheme had then been specified for Air Force Phantoms, so the first fighter and reconnaissance variants received by the Air Force were painted in the same scheme as the Navy and Marine aircraft. At that time, a gray over white paint scheme was specified for Navy and Marine fighters. Light Gull Gray (FS 36440) was applied to most upper surfaces, while the undersides of the aircraft were white. Both upper and lower surfaces of the flaps and ailerons were white, as were both sides of the rudder. The outer panels of the horizontal stabilators were also white on both the top and bottom surfaces, while the inner panels were natural metal.

Although early RF-4Cs were assigned to operational Air Force squadrons in this paint scheme, very little, if

It wasn't long after the Air Force placed the RF-4C in operation that the Standard camouflage scheme was developed. The undersides were a very light gray, while the upper surfaces were painted in a pattern of two greens and a tan. This aircraft is from the 67th TRW, and it was photographed at Luke AFB, Arizona, on 21 September, 1976. (Malerba)

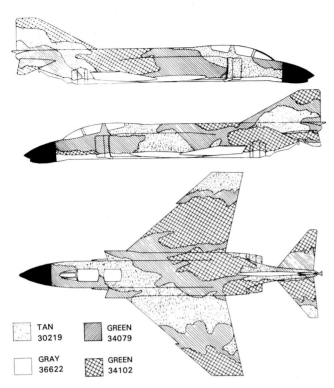

TAN 30219	GREEN 34079
GRAY 36622	GREEN 34102

The official drawing from Technical Order 1-1-4 for the Standard camouflage scheme was drawn for an F-4C variant. However, the colors on the nose were just extended for the RF-4C, with the rest of the pattern remaining the same as shown here. **(USAF)**

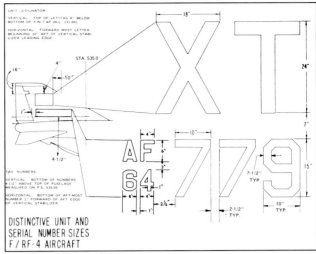

DISTINCTIVE UNIT AND SERIAL NUMBER SIZES F/RF-4 AIRCRAFT

The specifications for applying tail codes and serial numbers to Air Force Phantoms are shown in this official drawing. **(USAF)**

any, unit markings were ever applied to these aircraft. A few RF-4Cs flew combat missions in Vietnam in the gray over white scheme, but again there was almost a total lack of any unit markings on these Phantoms.

Shortly after hostilities commenced in Southeast Asia, the Air Force developed what became known as the Standard camouflage scheme. Technical Order 1-1-4 directed that two greens (FS 34079 and 34102) and a tan (FS 30219) be applied in a specific pattern to the upper surfaces and sides of the aircraft. A very light gray (FS 36622) was to be painted on the undersurfaces. As was the case with most combat aircraft in the Air Force's inventory, a pattern using these colors was designed specifically for the Phantom. Technical Order 1-1-4 did not differentiate between the different Phantom variants. The drawing used in the tech order was of an F-4C, however the same pattern was intended for use on the

RF-4C as well. The only change required was to extend the camouflage scheme further forward on the RF-4C's elongated nose section.

When the Standard camouflage scheme first appeared on operational aircraft, **USAF** and the serial number was stencilled in small black letters on each side of the vertical tail. But this was soon replaced with tail codes which were painted in white letters that were twenty-four inches high. Beneath the tail code an **AF** and an abbreviated serial number was stencilled. Usually, the **AF** and the last two digits of the contract year were stencilled in black characters that were six inches in height. The **AF** was on top, and the two numbers were beneath it. This was followed by the last three or four numbers of the serial number which were fifteen inches high and painted white.

After the war in Vietnam, there was a shift toward low visibility markings. The white tail codes and serial numbers were changed to black, and the tri-colored national insignias were replaced with ones that were nothing more than black stencils.

The Standard camouflage scheme began to be replaced by the Wraparound camouflage scheme in the mid-to-late 1970s. The same two greens and the tan used in the Standard scheme remained in use for the Wraparound scheme, but the pattern of these three colors was also extended to the lower surfaces of the aircraft as well. Thus, the use of the light gray was discontinued. Techni-

This in-flight photograph of an RF-4C from the 160th TFS of the Alabama Air National Guard illustrates how the two greens and the tan of the Standard camouflage scheme were "wrapped around" on to the undersides of the aircraft to make the Wraparound camouflage scheme.
(Spering/A.I.R.)

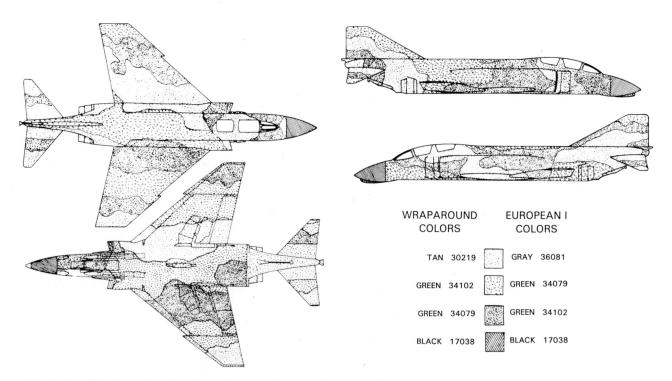

WRAPAROUND COLORS		EUROPEAN I COLORS
TAN 30219		GRAY 36081
GREEN 34102		GREEN 34079
GREEN 34079		GREEN 34102
BLACK 17038		BLACK 17038

This is the official drawing for the pattern used on the Wraparound and European I camouflage schemes. Color keys are provided for each scheme. Again, an F-4C was used as the basis for the drawing, but the pattern was just carried a little more forward on the nose section of the RF-4C. Note how the patterns for the sides and undersurfaces do not line up. It would be impossible to paint an aircraft exactly like this drawing, so there was a lot of variation when it came to painting the actual aircraft. (USAF)

cal Order 1-1-4 specified a pattern for the undersides of Phantoms, however, this pattern did not match what was on the sides of the fuselage. Therefore, it was impossible to follow the tech order, and this resulted in some significantly different patterns being applied to the undersides of the aircraft.

The next scheme to appear on Air Force Phantoms was the European I camouflage scheme. This scheme used the same pattern as the Wraparound scheme, however the colors were changed. Both greens (FS 34079 and 34102) were still used, but they were in different locations within the pattern. The tan was deleted, and gray (FS 36081) became the third color in this scheme. For the most part, low visibility markings remained the norm, but some color did appear, especially when aircraft participated in special competitions.

The European I camouflage scheme used the same pattern as the Wraparound scheme. However, as explained in the text, the colors were different. The European I scheme is shown to good effect on this RF-4C from the 67th TRW as it made its approach for landing. (Grove)

In what was perhaps the most attractive camouflage scheme ever applied to Air Force Phantoms, the grays used on the F-16 were applied to many F-4s late in their service life. In some cases, all three grays used on the F-16 were also used on the Phantoms in what was known as the Hill Gray I scheme. However, in most cases, particularly with the RF-4C, only the dark and medium grays were used. This two-tone gray scheme was known as Hill Gray II. F-4C, 66-0467, shows off a new Hill Gray II scheme and colorful markings in January 1989. This was the commander's aircraft for the 67th Tactical Reconnaissance wing at that time. (Greby)

The last paint scheme that has been applied to Air Force Phantoms, including the RF-4C, uses the same grays found in the camouflage scheme designed for the F-16. The original design used all three grays (FS 36118, 36270, and 36375), and it was initially known as the Hill Gray scheme. Then a second design was developed which used only two of the grays, and this was known as the Hill Gray II scheme. To differentiate between the two variations, the original three-tone scheme then became known as the Hill Gray I scheme. During Operations Desert Shield and Desert Storm RF-4Cs were painted in the Hill Gray II scheme.

The official directive for the Hill Gray II scheme states that the darker gray is to be Gunship Gray (36118), and the lighter of the two grays is to be Medium Gray (36270). Scale modelers should note that instruction sheets for a kit and an after-market decal sheet have indicated that the lighter of the two grays used on RF-4Cs assigned to the Alabama Air National Guard's 106th Reconnaissance Squadron was 36320 instead of 36270. This is incorrect. We checked with the 106th RS during the preparation of this book and were told that the lighter gray that they use is 36270 as called for in the directive. Unit personnel stated that 36320 has never been used on their aircraft, and they said further that they did not even have any of that color on hand.

*The undersides of an RF-4C painted in the Hill Gray II scheme are illustrated in this excellent in-flight photograph. Note how the dark gray extends well forward on the nose. This is the same aircraft as shown on the front cover and on page 39. The well known Phantom "Spook" can be seen on the centerline tank with a **35** on his costume to commemorate the thirty-fifth anniversary of the Phantom's first flight. **1958** and **1993** are also painted on the tank to indicate the span of thirty-five years since the first F-4 took to the air.* (Spering/A.I.R.)

Air Force Phantoms used by test and evaluation units and for other special purposes often have non-standard paint schemes. In most cases, these aircraft are painted overall white, and have high-visibility markings. This RF-4C is from the 6512th Test Squadron, and its **ED** tail code is derived from Edwards AFB, California. Note the high-visibility red markings on the vertical tail, the horizontal stabilators, and the wings.

(Grove)

Phantom 12200 was the first YRF-4C prototype, and it also served as the YF-4E prototype. It was involved in numerous test and evaluation programs, and is now on display at the U. S. Air Force Museum at Dayton, Ohio. It was tested with a fly-by-wire system and canard wings, and these remain in place as seen in this photograph. It has an overall white paint scheme with a blue flash that runs the length of the fuselage.

(Kinzey)

Marine RF-4Bs were originally delivered in the Light Gull Gray over white paint scheme as seen on this aircraft from VMFP-3. The undersides of the aircraft are white, and the demarcation between the white and light gull gray can be seen on the lower nose section in this photograph. The rudder is white, as are the outer panels of the horizontal stabilizers. The upper surfaces of the flaps and ailerons are also white, however this is difficult to see from this angle. The markings are rather colorful, and the entire vertical tail has been painted with squadron colors. The national insignias are large and are red, white, and blue. (Leslie)

The second official paint scheme used on Marine RF-4Bs was the overall Light Gull Gray scheme. At first, colorful markings often remained, as did the large colorful national insignias. In other cases, as on the aircraft shown here, the markings were all painted black, and sometimes even the national insignias were large black or gray stencils.   (Kinzey)

The forty-six RF-4Bs that were delivered to the Marines were originally painted in the Light Gull Gray over white scheme as explained above. After the war in Vietnam, the Navy and Marines also started a move to lower visibility for their aircraft. The overall gray scheme replaced the gray over white scheme, and this was accomplished simply by painting the entire aircraft Light Gull Gray. The white on the undersides and the control surfaces was deleted. For a short time, large colorful markings remained the norm on the overall gray scheme, but these were gradually replaced with low visibility markings using mostly black and different shades of gray.

The overall gray scheme remained in effect until near the end of the RF-4B's service life. Some remaining aircraft with VMFP-3 were painted in a tactical paint scheme which used two different shades of gray. Photographs and research indicate that the grays used on various aircraft differed considerably, and it is not possible to provide Federal Standard numbers which were applicable to all RF-4Bs painted in this scheme.

The final two RF-4Bs in service received special markings for a retirement ceremony. One was painted overall gloss black and had white markings, while the other was painted overall gloss Light Gull Gray (FS 16440) and had multi-colored markings. Photographs of these two aircraft can be found on page 64.

Near the end of their service life, some RF-4Bs were painted in what was known as a tactical camouflage scheme. It consisted of two grays as shown here, however the two shades of gray often varied from one aircraft to another. The national insignias were reduced in size, and all markings were either black or gray. This photograph was taken in November 1986.
(Grove)

10th TACTICAL RECONNAISSANCE WING

The 10th Tactical Reconnaissance Wing was based at Alconbury Air Base, England, and in April 1965 it became one of the first units to receive RF-4Cs. This photograph shows 64-1014 while it was still in the gray over white scheme, and as was typical for Phantoms in this early scheme, it carries no unit markings. Note the buzz number on the side of the fuselage, and the camouflaged drop tank under the right wing.

(Military Aircraft Photographs)

At left is a view of RF-4C, 64-1009, that illustrates the change to the Standard camouflage scheme. The **AS** tail code was assigned to aircraft of the 30th Tactical Reconnaissance Squadron as was the yellow and black tail band. At right is a close-up of the 10th TRW insignia as used on the aircraft. *(Flightleader collection)*

This photograph of RF-4C, 64-1006, illustrates that the squadron insignia was applied to the left side of the aircraft. By the time this photograph was taken in 1971, the 30th TRS had changed to a red fin cap.
(Military Aircraft Photographs)

*The 32nd TRS used the **AT** tail code and a yellow tail band when this photograph of 64-1069 was taken in 1971. (Military Aircraft Photographs)*

*Originally, the 1st Tactical Reconnaissance Squadron used the **AR** tail code, but in 1972, all squadrons in the 10th TRW were assigned this code as the wing maintenance concept was adopted. The different colored tail bands indicated the squadron to which each aircraft was assigned. This Phantom had a blue fin cap representing the 32nd TRS. (Flightleader collection)*

RF-4C, 68-0564, is being checked over prior to a training flight. The change to black tail codes and serial numbers can be seen in this photograph taken in late 1980. (de Kruyff)

This Phantom was a participant at Best Focus '82, as indicated by the special markings on the nose. The change to the Wraparound scheme is evidenced by this photograph dated July 1982. (Flightleader collection)

The 10th TRW had changed to the European I scheme when this RF-4C was photographed in April 1984. (GB Aircraft Slides)

RF-4C, 68-0567, carries special markings that designate it as the wing commander's aircraft. Notice the shadowed treatment of the tail markings, the checkerboard band applied to the lower portion of the nose, and the anti-glare panel that wraps around the nose. The 10th TRW was redesignated the 10th Tactical Fighter Wing in August 1987 and began a transition to the A-10 Warthog before the Hill Gray II scheme was painted on its RF-4Cs. (Mills)

18th TACTICAL FIGHTER WING

The 18th TFW became one of four tactical fighter wings to operate RF-4Cs when the 15th Tactical Reconnaissance Squadron was assigned to it in 1967. The unit was based at Kadena AB, Okinawa and used the *ZZ* tail code on their aircraft. This Phantom was photographed in May 1972, and it displays a yellow and black checkerboard band on its fin cap.

(Gilliss via Rotramel)

The view of RF-4C, 66-0397, illustrates the markings applied to the left side of the aircraft. The wing badge is located on the engine inlet. (Nishimura)

By the time this photograph was taken in September 1988, the 15th TRS had changed to the European I camouflage scheme and was using low visibility markings on its aircraft. However, the yellow and black tail band remained in color. Notice the Shogun warrior painted in gray just forward of the wing badge. (Whited)

Some of the more colorful markings that were used on the European I camouflage scheme were added for photo reconnaissance competitions. These markings were used by the 18th TFW in late 1985. (Whited)

RF-4C, 68-0582, was photographed at a photo reconnaissance meet in 1986. Compare these different markings to the ones shown above. The 18th TFW gave up its RF-4Cs prior to the introduction of the Hill Gray II paint scheme. (Grove)

26th TACTICAL RECONNAISSANCE WING

The 26th Tactical Reconnaissance Wing was based at Ramstein AB, Germany, and its squadrons flew a variety of aircraft. The first of its squadrons to operate the RF-4C was the 38th Tactical Reconnaissance Squadron, and this unit used **RR** tail codes on its aircraft. This photograph shows one of the unit's RF-4Cs as it appeared in 1971. Of interest are the numerous zaps on the inlet ramp and below the cockpit. Also note the shark's mouth painted on the nose.
(Military Aircraft Photographs)

This right side view of RF-4C, 65-0824, illustrates the typical markings used by the 38th TRS in 1971. The wing badge was applied to the right inlet. (Military Aircraft Photographs)

The 17th Tactical Reconnaissance Squadron was added to 26th TRW after it moved to Zweibrucken AB, Germany. One of its Phantoms is shown here with special markings for a Royal Flush photo competition.
(Centurion Enterprises)

During Royal Flush '75, one of the aircraft from the 17th TRS was photographed while being prepared for a flight. Compare this marking with the one seen on the previous page for an earlier Royal Flush photo meet.

(Knowles collection)

This Phantom was photographed while taxiing out for a mission during a tactical air meet in 1982. Notice the small shark's mouth painted on the aircraft. By this time, the 26th TRW had changed to the Wraparound camouflage scheme and used low visibility markings on its aircraft.

(Flightleader collection)

This right front view of RF-4C, 71-0254, depicts the typical low visibility markings applied to aircraft of the 26th TRW. The obvious exception is the small shark's mouth. *(GB Aircraft Slides)*

The European I camouflage scheme had been applied to this Phantom by August 1985. All markings were flat black. *(Flightleader collection)*

The 26th TRW had changed to the Hill Gray II scheme by the time Operations Desert Shield and Desert Storm began. This RF-4C carried an Iraqi flag and three and one-half mission markings on the inlet ramp. Kodak film logos were used for the mission markings. This is the wing commander's aircraft as indicated by the special markings on the tail. Also note the green and white bands on the tail and engine inlet. *(Flightleader collection)*

67th TACTICAL RECONNAISSANCE WING

The 67th Tactical Reconnaissance Wing began its transition to the RF-4C at Mountain Home AFB, Idaho, in January 1966. At that time, the Air Force was under the squadron maintenance concept, and each squadron had its own tail code. Aircraft assigned to the 7th Tactical Reconnaissance Squadron used the **KT** tail code as shown in this photograph dated 18 April, 1970.

(Morris via Lock)

This Phantom was photographed in 1969 while it was assigned to the 10th TRS. This squadron used **KR** as its tail code, and the fin cap was yellow. (Military Aircraft Photographs)

The 22nd TRS used the **KS** tail code, and the fin caps on its aircraft were blue with a white shooting star.
(Military Aircraft Photographs)

By the time this photograph was taken in December 1975, the 67th TRW had moved to Bergstrom AFB, Texas, and adopted the **BA** tail code for all squadrons in the wing. This aircraft also sported a sinister shark's mouth on its nose.
(Logan)

This Phantom carried small bi-centennial markings in the form of a red, white, and blue fin cap, and the bi-centennial pretzel was placed on the fuselage. (Slowiak)

This RF-4C was photographed at an air show at Holloman AFB, New Mexico, in November 1982. By that time, the 67th TRW had changed to Wrap-around camouflage scheme and low visibility markings. (Kinzey)

The commander's aircraft for the 67th TRW was RF-4C, 66-0467, when this photograph was taken in August 1985. It was painted in European I camouflage, however it had a colorful wing badge, multi-colored fin cap, and a black and white tail code. The wing's designation was also painted on the tail in shadowed letters. (Wilson)

The commander's aircraft for the 12th TRS was painted in the Hill Gray II scheme and had colorful wing and TAC badges. The fin cap was bright red, and the **BA** and **12TRS** were black with a white shadow. (Leavitt)

The last flight of an RF-4C from the 67th TRW took place on 1 September, 1992. The event was commemorated with a hand-written inscription on the nose of 68-0565. (Flightleader collection)

75th TACTICAL RECONNAISSANCE WING

The 75th Tactical Reconnaissance Wing preceded the 67th TRW at Bergstrom AFB, Texas. This Phantom was assigned to the 91st TRS, and was photographed on 27 May, 1970. At that time, the 91st TRS was using the **BA** tail code.
(Lock)

At left is a view of RF-4C, 68-0589, when it was assigned to the 4th TRS. This squadron used the **BB** tail code. At right is an aircraft from the 9th TRS which was assigned the **BC** tail code. (Left Malerba, right Ostrowski)

86th TACTICAL FIGHTER WING

The 86th Tactical Fighter Wing had the 17th TRS as an assigned unit when that squadron was equipped with RF-4Cs. The **ZR** tail code was allocated only to the 17th TRS until wing codes took over in 1972. After that time, the entire 86th TFW used this tail code. This photograph of RF-4C, 68-0558, was taken in 1971.
(Military Aircraft Photographs)

363rd TACTICAL RECONNAISSANCE WING

The 363rd Tactical Reconnaissance Wing was based at Shaw AFB, South Carolina. The 16th TRS became the first of its squadrons to receive RF-4C Phantoms in June 1965, and it was followed by the 4415th Combat Crew Training Squadron in early 1967 and the 18th TRS in 1970. When the Air Force used squadron-level tail codes, the 16th TRS adopted the *JM* code after returning from a combat tour in Southeast Asia. An example of one of this unit's aircraft can be seen in the top left photograph. The 18th TRS used *JP* as seen above, and the 4415th was assigned the letters *JL* as shown at left.

(All Military Aircraft Photographs)

When the change was made to wing-level tail codes, the 363rd TRW adopted the *JO* code for all of its aircraft. Meanwhile, the 4414th CCTS was redesignated the 33rd TRTS, and the 22nd TRS was added to the wing. The 22nd TRS was then replaced by the 62nd TRS in late 1971. This RF-4C was the wing commander's aircraft when this photograph was taken at Andrews AFB, Maryland, on 21 May, 1977. The multi-colored fin cap represented each of the squadrons within the wing.

(Zinc)

The change to the Wraparound camouflage scheme and black tail codes is illustrated on this RF-4C that was photographed in February 1981. Reconnaissance Phantoms often operated with ECM pods. *(Flightleader)*

363rd TACTICAL FIGHTER WING

*The 363rd TRW was redesignated as the 363rd Tactical Fighter Wing in 1982 as it prepared to transition to F-16s. A new **SW** tail code was adopted and was derived from the first and last letters of Shaw AFB where the unit was stationed. The 16th TRS continued to operate the RF-4C until late 1989, and 69-0363 was painted in special markings for the wing commander when this photograph was taken in December 1982.* (GB Aircraft Slides)

The 16th TRS had changed to the European I paint scheme when this aircraft was photographed in November 1986. The special markings on the tail would suggest this aircraft had participated in a reconnaissance air meet. (Grove)

The Phantoms of the 363rd TFW were changing over to the Hill Gray II paint scheme as they were phased out of service.
(Grove)

432nd TRW & 432nd TFW

The 432nd Tactical Reconnaissance Wing operated F-4D, F-4E, and RF-4C Phantoms out of Udorn RTAFB, Thailand, during the war in Vietnam. Phantom units from the United States were placed under its control during combat tours in Southeast Asia. Two Tactical Reconnaissance Squadrons were assigned to the wing, one of which was the 11th TRS. RF-4C, 65-905, was operated by this squadron as indicated by the unit's **OO** tail code and black fin cap.
(Centurion Enterprises)

The other RF-4C squadron to operate with the 432nd TRW was the 14th TRS, and this unit used white **OZ** tail codes. Notice the Playboy bunny painted in white on the inlet ramp and the small shark's mouth on the nose of this RF-4C. By the time this photograph was taken in 1973, the 432nd TRW had been redesignated as the 432nd TFW. (Gilliss via Rotramel)

460th TACTICAL RECONNAISSANCE WING

*The 460th Tactical Reconnaissance Wing was assigned to Tan Son Nhut AB, RSVN, and two RF-4C squadrons were among its several units. These included the 16th TRS and 12th TRS. While in SEA, the 16th TRS used an **AE** tail code, and the 12th TRS used **AC** as seen on this aircraft.* *(Flightleader collection)*

475th TACTICAL FIGHTER WING

*The 16th TRS was reassigned from the 460th TRW to the 475th TFW in 1970, and it was relocated to Misawa AB, Japan. Its Phantoms had **UE** tail codes while assigned to the 475th TFW, then changed to **JM** when they returned to the United States and their parent unit, the 363rd TRW. (See page 22.)* *(Military Aircraft Photographs)*

3247th TEST SQUADRON

The 3247th Test Squadron was part of the 3246th Test Wing at Eglin AFB, Florida. One of its RF-4Cs was photographed in November 1975, and it displays the typical markings used by the unit. The red diamonds on the white band stand out against the Aircraft Gray (FS 16473) paint scheme. This scheme was specified for many fighter variants of the Phantom when they were assigned to units with a primary air defense mission, but very few RF-4Cs were ever painted in this scheme. The Air Force Systems Test Command badge was applied to the fuselage. (Flightleader)

RF-4C, 69-0378, was also assigned to the 3247th Test Squadron, however it was painted in the Standard camouflage scheme. It was used for testing the Pave Tack system on the RF-4C. (Flightleader)

*The squadron had added the **AD** tail code to its aircraft by October 1982 when this photographed was taken. Although the fuel tanks still had the light gray undersides, the aircraft was painted in the Wraparound camouflage scheme.*
(Flightleader)

*The squadron was redesignated as the 3427th TESTS in 1989, and the tail code was change to **ET**. This RF-4C was painted in the Hill Gray II scheme and had contrasting gray markings. The two badges were still in color and the red diamonds on the white band remained on the tail.*
(Rankin-Lowe)

4485th TEST SQUADRON

Preceding the activation of the 4485th Test Squadron, RF-4Cs were assigned to the 4533rd Tactical Training Squadron (Test), which was a component of the 33rd TFW at Eglin AFB, Florida. Their RF-4Cs had the same **EG** tail code as the 33rd TFW. RF--4C, 65-0843, was photographed at Eglin AFB on 4 May, 1971. *(Lock)*

The 4485th TS then replaced the 4533rd TTS (Test), and between 1978 and 1982, this unit operated RF-4Cs with **ED** tail codes. The same tail code was also being used on aircraft assigned to the 33rd TFW during that time frame. Notice the 33rd TFW badge on the fuselage and the LORAN antenna on the spine. *(Flightleader)*

By 1982, the 4485th TS had changed to the **OT** tail code and a black and white checkerboard tail band had been added to its aircraft. This RF-4C was painted in the Wraparound camouflage scheme and had black markings. (Bracken)

RF-4C, 64-1028, was painted in the European I scheme with black markings when this photograph was taken at Eglin AFB, in May 1986. Note the ALQ-131 ECM pod on the right inboard pylon. (Flightleader)

The 4485th TS had adopted the new Hill Gray II paint scheme when this aircraft was photographed at the London International Air Show on 3 June, 1988.
(Flightleader)

4490th TEST GROUP

The 4490th Test Group was part of the Air Force Special Weapons Center at Kirtland AFB, New Mexico, and it also operated a number of Phantoms. Here is another rare example of an RF-4C that was painted in the overall Aircraft Gray scheme, and it appears that the side camera window has been painted over. The tail band was orange with yellow triangles. Note the camouflaged fuel tank under the left wing.
(Flightleader collection)

6510th TEST WING

The 6510th Test Wing is based at Edwards AFB, California, and it also operated several Phantoms for various test projects. RF-4C, 65-0850, was photographed while making an approach for landing, and it displays typical markings used by this unit. The **ED** tail codes were accompanied by a blue tail band with white Xs, and it was edged in white.

(Grove)

The wing also had Phantoms painted overall white with high-visibility markings. The **ED** tail codes were black.

(Kaston)

OGDEN AIR LOGISTICS CENTER

The Ogden Air Logistics Center is located at Hill AFB, Utah. As the primary rework center for the F-4, it had examples of each type of Phantom assigned on which it could evaluate proposed airframe modifications. RF-4C, 63-7744, is in the overall white scheme with high-visibility red panels on the wings and tail, but it carries no specific markings for the Ogden ALC.

(Picciani Aircraft Slides)

RF-4C, 65-0905, has a large **HAFB** across the tail which stands for Hill Air Force Base.

(Flightleader)

ALABAMA AIR NATIONAL GUARD
106th RECONNAISSANCE SQUADRON

The 106th TRS of 117th TRW is part of the Alabama ANG, and this popular unit has operated the RF-4C for many years. They will soon be re-equipped with KC-135s to end an important chapter of tactical reconnaissance history. The unit is based in Birmingham, Alabama, and it has been one of the most colorful recon Phantom operators. This is one of the unit's earliest RF-4Cs, and it is painted in the Standard camouflage scheme. The Air National Guard's bi-centennial insignia is on the nose. *(Campbell)*

This Phantom was photographed on 13 June, 1980, at Nellis AFB, Nevada, as it participated in a Red Flag exercise. Notice the yellow fin cap and the ECM pod on the wing pylon. *(Flightleader)*

This Phantom was painted in the Wraparound camouflage scheme when it was photographed at Dobbins AFB, Georgia, on 6 September, 1982.
(Flightleader)

The unit later changed to the European I camouflage scheme as shown here. This aircraft has an unusual green fin cap.
(Grove)

DESERT STORM MARKINGS

After changing to the Hill Gray II scheme and adding the **BH** tail code which was derived from Birmingham, RF-4Cs from the 106th TRS were deployed to the Middle East for Operations Desert Shield and Desert Storm. These aircraft provided valuable reconnaissance while being flown by pilots from both the Alabama and Nevada Air National Guard units. RF-4C, 65-0833, was one of the aircraft that participated in the Gulf War, and it displays a colorful shark's mouth on its nose. Other aircraft had low-visibility shark's mouths that were painted in contrasting shades of gray.
(Flightleader)

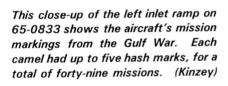

This close-up of the left inlet ramp on 65-0833 shows the aircraft's mission markings from the Gulf War. Each camel had up to five hash marks, for a total of forty-nine missions. (Kinzey)

At left is the right side of RF-4C, 64-0033, which was another aircraft that participated in Desert Shield and Desert Storm. At right is a close-up of the markings on the left side of the nose. **90, 91, DESERT STORM, SLEEPER,** and the top of the palm tree were painted pale green and were edged with black. **DESERT SHIELD** was painted brown and outlined with black. The other lettering was black to include the outline of the state of Nevada and the **412 UNIT SORTIES.**
(Both Kinzey)

The 106th TRS participated in Reconnaissance Air Meet '86 at Bergstrom AFB, Texas. One of its Phantoms was photographed while waiting for the next mission on 2 November, 1986. Note the yellow stars on the fin cap.

(Rogers)

After returning from the Middle East, the 106th TRS added **ALABAMA** in yellow to the fin caps of its aircraft. This photograph shows the flight line at Birmingham in the fall of 1991.

(Kinzey)

This close-up shows the new markings applied to the fin caps. **ALABAMA** is in yellow and is edged with a thin black outline. A tail band, which is nothing more than a black outline, is just in front of and behind the state's name. The serial number is also edged in black, but is painted Gunship Gray. This is the squadron commander's aircraft, and notice that this photograph was taken after the word "tactical" had been dropped from the designations for the wing and the squadron.

(Kinzey)

117th TRW & 117th RW COMMANDER'S AIRCRAFT

When the RF-4C reached the twenty year mark of service with the 117th TRW, the commander's aircraft was painted with these special markings. The left side of RF-4C, 65-0854, is shown here as it appeared on 14 August, 1992. *1971 TWENTY YEARS OF PHANTOMS 1991* was painted on the fuselage spine in red and white letters.   (Flightleader)

A view of the right side of the same aircraft shows that *1971 BIRMINGHAM RECCE REBELS 1991* was painted in red and white letters on this side of the spine.
(Flightleader)

The wing badge was painted on both inlets, and the insignias of other recon Phantom units surrounded it. The famous Phantom "Spook" character stood atop the wing badge.   (Kinzey)

This close-up of the travel pod was taken after the word "tactical" had been deleted from the wing's designation.   (Kinzey)

DIAMOND JUBILEE AIRCRAFT

Most of the fancy artwork painted on the aircraft of the 106th TRS was done by Don Spering of Aircraft In Review. He received the cooperation of General James Brown, former commanding officer of the 117th RW. The pride and southern hospitality of General Brown and the 117th RW is well known in aviation circles. This aircraft was painted for the unit's Diamond Jubilee. **106TH RECCE REBELS 1917 JENNIES TO JETS 1992** is written in red and white letters on the spine. This indicated that the unit began its flying operations in Jenny biplanes at the end of World War I, and now flies jets seventy-five years later. *(Flightleader)*

The markings on the left side of 65-0843 are seen in this photograph which illustrates that **DIAMOND JUBILEE** was substituted in place of **JENNIES TO JETS** on this side of the aircraft. *(Flightleader)*

This close-up shows the markings on the right side of the nose of the Diamond Jubilee Phantom. *(Flightleader)*

The nose markings on the left side of the aircraft are seen here. Notice the mission markings on the splitter plate. **RECCE REBELS** was painted above the artwork and consisted of a Confederate soldier riding on an RF-4C. *(Kinzey)*

35th ANNIVERSARY AIRCRAFT

Another Phantom painted in special markings by Don Spering celebrates of the 35th anniversary of the Phantom's first flight. This beautiful in-flight photograph illustrates the markings painted on the right side of the aircraft. Before Don added the special markings, the unit repainted this aircraft using semi-gloss paint instead of the usual flat finish. Therefore the Gunship Gray was 26118 instead of 36118, and the lighter shade of gray was 26270 instead of 36370. A Confederate soldier is on this side of the rudder. (Spering/A.I.R.)

The left side of the same aircraft displays its proud colors in this photograph. On this side of the rudder is the Phantom "Spook" character. Notice the markings on the travel pod, and the flags of the various nations that have flown Phantoms. An underside view of this aircraft is on page 7, and it reveals the artwork painted on the centerline fuel tank. (Spering/A.I.R.)

ALABAMA AIR NATIONAL GUARD
160th TACTICAL FIGHTER SQUADRON

The 160th TRS of the 187th TRG was the second unit of the Alabama Air National Guard that operated RF-4Cs. It was based at Dannelly Field ANGB, in Montgomery. One of its early Phantoms is seen in this photograph taken in April 1978. **ALABAMA** was painted on the fin cap in white.
(Flightleader)

*RF-4C, 63-0756, was photographed as it taxied out for a mission. Notice the squadron badge on the fuselage and the change to **MONTGOMERY** in white letters on the red fin cap.*
(Flightleader)

*The fin cap was later painted white with **MONTGOMERY** being lettered in red. A zap in the form of a black Armadillo had been painted on the splitter plate during a visit to Texas.*
(Flightleader)

This photograph illustrates two different fin caps. The closer aircraft has a blue cap with gold letters, and the aircraft in the background has a red cap with gold letters. Silver was not used for **Montgomery** *as provided on some after-market decal sheets for modelers.* (Flightleader)

Two of Montgomery's Phantoms participated in a reconnaissance meet in Europe during 1980. The special tail markings used during that competition can be seen in this photograph. (Greve)

The 160th TRS later changed to the Wraparound camouflage scheme and low visibility black markings. However, the red and gold fin cap remained. This unit transitioned to F-4Ds not long after this photograph was taken, and it now operates F-16 Falcons.
(Flightleader)

CALIFORNIA AIR NATIONAL GUARD

A latecomer to recon Phantoms was the 196th TRS of 163rd TRG. This unit is assigned to the California Air National Guard and is based at March AFB. The unit received their RF-4Cs in the Hill Gray II scheme, and squadron personnel added the same style tail band that had been used previously on its F-102s, O-2As, F-4Cs, and F-4Es. Note the red, white, and blue stripes at the top of the fin cap on this aircraft. (Huston)

RF-4C, 63-0762, was photographed in March 1990. The squadron was redesignated as the 196th RS of the 163rd RG, in 1992. The top of the fin cap on this aircraft is blue. (Huston)

IDAHO AIR NATIONAL GUARD

The 190th TRS of the 124th TRG is part of the Idaho Air National Guard, and it is based at Boise. This view of RF-4C, 65-0924, illustrates the markings on the unit's aircraft in 1977.   (Knowles)

The squadron won first place at Photo Finish '83 and marked the rudder of its aircraft to indicate the accomplishment. Notice the glossy finish that was applied to the Wraparound camouflage scheme.   (Grove)

European I camouflage replaced the Wraparound scheme by May 1985. The gold tail band with **IDAHO** in blue was retained for a touch of color.
                    (MacPherson)

The Idaho ANG later changed to the Hill Gray II scheme as illustrated in this photograph of RF-4C, 66-0923.
(Soulaine)

At left is a view of 65-0874, which is also in the Hill Gray II scheme. At right is a close-up of the markings used on the fin cap of the unit's aircraft. The mountains and **IDAHO** are painted in blue against a gold band.
(Left Flightleader, right Kaston)

ILLINOIS AIR NATIONAL GUARD

The 170th TFS of the 183rd TFG was assigned to the Illinois ANG and based at Springfield. Although it primarily flew F-4Cs and F-4Ds, it also operated two RF-4Cs for a time. One of those two aircraft, 65-0875, is shown here as it appeared in June 1975. Notice the unusual green fin cap on this aircraft.
(Jenkins)

KENTUCKY AIR NATIONAL GUARD

The 165th TRS of 123rd TRW was part of the Kentucky Air National Guard and was based at Louisville. The unit converted from RF-101H Voodoos to RF-4Cs in early 1976. One of their Phantoms shows the early markings with **KY** painted in white above the ANG badge. This photograph is dated 18 December, 1976. *(Flightleader)*

By August 1980, a more colorful fin cap had been added to Kentucky's recon Phantoms. **KENTUCKY** was painted in blue on the white cap, and small red, white, and blue stripes were added below it. *(Flightleader)*

By 1982 the unit had painted its aircraft in the Wraparound scheme. Low visibility black markings were used except that the colorful fin cap was retained. The **KY** tail code was added to the tail. *(Flightleader)*

Photo Derby '82 saw the addition of special markings on the rudder of the Kentucky Air National Guard's aircraft. The small red, white, and blue stripes below the fin cap can also be seen. *(GB Aircraft Slides)*

The 106th TRS also participated in a European reconnaissance meet during 1982. The words **BEST FOCUS 82** were painted in white below the three flags on the fuselage. Also note the colorful markings on the rudder of the aircraft. *(GB Aircraft Slides)*

At left is an overall view of RF-4C, 64-1071, which is painted in the European I scheme. At right is a close-up of the colorful markings on the fin cap. *(Both Kinzey)*

Reconnaissance air meets usually brought out colorful markings and the competitive spirit of most units. Kentucky was no exception as evidenced by the nice markings painted on the tail of this Phantom. They almost make a European I paint scheme acceptable!

(Grove)

The Kentucky ANG changed over to the Hill Gray II paint scheme in 1986. The fin cap was still white with two small red stripes, but the other markings were black or gray. (Grove)

At left is an overall view of 65-0873, which is also painted in the Hill Gray II scheme. All markings are in a contrasting gray. At right is a close-up of the wing badge with the name **AMALGAM WARRIOR** stencilled at the top of the badge.

(Both Arrington)

MINNESOTA AIR NATIONAL GUARD

The 179th TRS of the 148th TRG was assigned to the Minnesota ANG and based at Duluth. This unit flew RF-4Cs from late 1975 until 1983. An example of its early markings can be seen on 64-1076 which was photographed in July 1976. **(Slowiak)**

*By 1980, the 179th TRS had moved **MINNESOTA** from the rear fuselage and placed it on the yellow fin cap in black letters.* **(Slowiak)**

*These are the final markings used by the 179th TRS before converting to F-4Ds in 1983. The fin cap was red, edged with white. **MINNESOTA** was in black letters that were outlined in yellow. The RF-4Cs were transferred out of the unit while still in the Wrap-around scheme.* **(Rogers)**

MISSISSIPPI AIR NATIONAL GUARD

The 153rd TRS of the 186th TRG is assigned to the Mississippi ANG. It started flying the RF-4C in 1978 from Key Field, and because of the name of its base, it adopted the *KE* tail code. This Phantom was photographed in October 1981, and it displays the early markings used by this unit. The *KE* tail code slightly overlapped the green and gold markings.   (Campbell)

This photograph was taken about the same time as the one above and illustrates the change to the Wraparound paint scheme on unit's Phantoms.
(Military Aircraft Photographs)

The 153rd TRS later change to the European I paint scheme, but there was only a slight change in the tail markings from those shown above. ***MISSISSIPPI MAGNOLIA MILITIA*** was added to the wing tanks.   (Rogers)

*The Mississippi ANG more recently painted their aircraft in the Hill Gray II scheme. The gray **MISSISSIPPI** and the serial numbers were edged in gold and contrasted nicely against the gray background.* *(Flightleader)*

This Phantom received special markings to commemorate the unit's fiftieth anniversary. The colorful magnolia on the tail was symbolic of the unit's nickname, "Magnolia Militia." *(Select Air Productions)*

NEBRASKA AIR NATIONAL GUARD

The Nebraska ANG has the 173rd TRS of the 155th TRG as one of its assigned units. This squadron has operated the RF-4C from their home base at Lincoln since early 1972. At left is an overall view of 65-0932 in the early markings used by this unit. **NEBR** was painted on the fin cap in white, and the unit's insignia was applied to the right engine inlet. At right is a close-up of the tail of 64-0998, revealing that **NEBR** was also painted in black on some aircraft.

(Both Flightleader)

The unit had changed to the Wraparound scheme by 1982 when this photograph was taken, and some colorful green and gold markings had been added to the rudder and fin cap. Note also the "Spook" Phantom II character on the inlet ramp.

(GB Aircraft Slides)

The European I scheme had replaced the Wraparound camouflage on Nebraska's Phantoms by 1986. The bright green also disappeared from the rudder and fin cap. The remaining markings were gold.

(Greby)

The Lincoln aircraft later were painted in the Hill Gray II scheme, and all markings were in a contrasting dark or light gray.

(Prettyman)

By 1988, a change had been made to the markings used on the fin cap of Nebraska's aircraft. **Nebraska** and two horizontal stripes were added in yellow. **LINCOLN** and the star were removed from the rudder.

(Flightleader collection)

This Phantom was a visitor to the London International Air Show on 2 June, 1988, and it displays another change in the markings on the fin cap. **Huskers** *is in dark gray between two blue lines.* (Flightleader)

Yet another variation to the tail markings was seen on RF-4C, 65-0932, in 1991. The unit also added the squadron badge in red to the forward fuselage. (Aviation Photography of Miami)

NEVADA AIR NATIONAL GUARD

The 192nd TRS of 152nd TRG is assigned to the Nevada ANG, and this unit has operated Phantoms from their base in Reno since 1975. Early markings included fin caps of several different colors with **NEVADA** in a contrasting color. This aircraft has a white fin cap with blue lettering and two red stars. *(Knowles)*

At left is an overall view of RF-4C, 64-1003. At right is a close-up of the black fin cap with white markings. *(Both Grove)*

This Phantom had **NEVADA** painted in black above the black ANG badge. Because this is difficult to see in the overall view at left, a close-up of the tail of another RF-4C with similar markings is provided at right. In this photo, the state's name is clearly visible above the ANG insignia. The stars in the white tail band are blue. *(Left Miller, right Grove)*

*More colorful markings were added to the unit's aircraft for Best Focus '76. Again, **NEVADA** was lettered above the ANG insignia, however this time it was in white, and the insignia was in full color rather than being a black stencil. Note the marking on the fuel tank.* *(Grove)*

*By 1981, several changes had been made to the markings on Nevada's Phantoms. The Standard camouflage scheme had been replaced with the Wraparound paint scheme. **RENO** had been added to the rudder, and **High Rollers** was painted across the fin cap. Red, white, and blue chevrons were also added to the vertical tail and wing tanks.* *(Grove)*

The 192nd TRS also used the European I paint scheme on its aircraft. The only unit markings were the white fin cap with **High Rollers** lettered in blue and **NEVADA** lettered in black above the ANG insignia. (Grove)

The Hill Gray II paint scheme was in use on Nevada's RF-4Cs by 1990. Colorful markings remained on the fin cap and the travel pod, and a special reconnaissance air meet badge was located on the fuselage. (Greby)

This close-up provides a look at the white fin cap with the red chevron and blue **High Rollers**. Note also that **NEVADA** remains above the ANG badge. (Flightleader)

VMCJ-1

Marine Composite Reconnaissance Squadron One (VMCJ-1) was based at MCAS Iwakuni, Japan, for most of the time it flew RF-4Bs. This recon Phantom was photographed on 28 August, 1975, and it was part of Detachment One aboard the USS MIDWAY. It was unusual to see pods on Navy or Marine Phantoms, but this RF-4C has an ALQ-88 on the left inboard wing pylon and an ALQ-81 on the right inboard pylon. *(Nishmura)*

Another RF-4B from VMCJ-1 was photographed while on static display. The aircraft did not have the dark green tail seen on the aircraft above, however all other markings were the same. The modex **15** indicates that this aircraft was assigned to MCAS Iwakuni.
(Flightleader collection)

Modex numbers in the **600** series replaced the usual two-digit nose numbers when Detachment One deployed aboard the USS Midway. However, the carrier's name was not painted on the aircraft. *(Nishimura)*

VMCJ-2

VMCJ-2 was another Marine composite reconnaissance squadron that operated RF-4Bs, and it was based at MCAS Cherry Point, North Carolina. The squadron was nicknamed "Playboys" and the Playboy bunny logo was painted on the rudder of its aircraft. This photograph of the squadron commander's aircraft was taken in 1977, and it illustrates the typical markings used by this unit.
(Flightleader collection)

Another RF-4B assigned to VMCJ-2 was 157344. This aircraft did not have the black tail shown above, but simply had the **CY** tail code painted in black.
(Flightleader collection)

VMCJ-3

VMCJ-3 was based at MCAS El Toro, California, until it transferred its Phantoms to VMFP-3 in mid 1975. One of their RF-4Cs shows the black **TN** tail code on a solid white vertical tail.   *(Lock)*

Another aircraft from VMCJ-3 is illustrated in this view of 153098. The chevron was painted green on these aircraft.   *(Flightleader collection)*

The left side of RF-4B, 153103, further illustrates the markings painted on VMCJ-3's aircraft.
          (Flightleader collection)

VMFP-3
LIGHT GULL GRAY OVER WHITE SCHEME

VMFP-3, which stands for Marine Tactical Reconnaissance Squadron Three, was formed in 1975 with aircraft from VMCJ-1, 2, and 3. This Phantom had a black tail with white markings. Originally known as "Eyes of the Corps," VMFP-3 then became the only unit equipped with RF-4Bs. The parent unit was stationed at El Toro MCAS, California, but detachments were located in Japan and Hawaii.

(Stewart)

This RF-4B was assigned to Detachment One at MCAS Iwakuni, Japan. The aircraft is painted in special markings for the American Bi-centennial. Note the name **USS MIDWAY** on the aft fuselage. The four-plane detachment in Japan often deployed aboard the MIDWAY when that carrier was based at Yokosuka.

(Nagakubo)

Another recon Phantom with special markings to celebrate America's two-hundredth birthday was RF-4B, 153101. Named **SPIRIT OF AMERICA**, it is shown here as it appeared in September 1976. Another photograph of this aircraft appears on the rear cover.

(Roth)

OVERALL LIGHT GULL GRAY SCHEME

One of the RF-4Bs assigned to the USS Midway from VMFP-3 was photographed on the carrier's flight deck in 1978. The aircraft was painted in the overall Light Gull Gray scheme and had simple black markings. *(Daniels)*

Another variation of VMFP-3's markings can be seen on this aircraft. Although they are a little more elaborate than the markings shown above, these are also simply black on the overall gray aircraft. *(Grove)*

VMFP-3 did use some color on the overall gray scheme. RF-4B, 153107, had a beautiful green tail with gold markings.
(Grove)

A combination of black and low visibility gray markings adorned this Phantom which was photographed on 26 July, 1980. Even the national insignias on this aircraft are gray.
(Flightleader)

All of the unit markings on this RF-4B were black. Notice the change to vertical *RF* tail codes and the "Spook" character on the tail. The national insignias are red, white, and blue, and the inlet warning is red and white.
(Flightleader)

TACTICAL PAINT SCHEME

VMFP-3 painted some of its Phantoms in a tactical gray scheme during their final years of service. These aircraft had a variety of contrasting gray markings. This RF-4B has a vertical **RF** tail code and the "Spook" character on the tail in dark gray.

(GB Aircraft Slides)

This Phantom had light gray markings on the tail. These included a lightning bolt, the "Spook" character, and a slanted **RF** tail code. *(Kinzey)*

This RF-4B was photographed at the London International Air Show and was painted in a tactical gray scheme with all black markings. Again, the markings are different from those shown on the aircraft at left or in the photo above. *(Flightleader)*

The Phantom pictured here had yet another variation of markings on the tactical gray colors. As pointed out on page 9, the grays used for the tactical schemes varied, and the two shades used on this aircraft are so close that it is hard to tell one from the other. It is also quite difficult to see the various markings except for the black **06** modex and the contrasting gray **RF** tail code.

(Flightleader collection)

RETIREMENT SCHEMES

VMFP-3 painted two aircraft in special markings for its deactivation ceremony that took place on 30 September, 1990. The last RF-4Bs were also retired on that date. This Phantom had a multi-colored tail to indicate that it was the Marine Aircraft Group II commander's aircraft. It was painted in the overall Light Gull Gray scheme.   *(Knowles)*

The other aircraft that was specially painted for the retirement and deactivation ceremony was RF-4B, 157351. It was overall gloss black and had white markings.
                                                                                    (Knowles)